W9-BDY-319

DOG OWNER'S GUIDE TO THE
Golden
Retriever

Bernard Bargh

FIREFLY BOOKS

A FIREFLY BOOK

Published by Firefly Books Ltd. 2005

Copyright © 2005 Ringpress Books Limited

All rights reserved. No part of this publication may be reproduced, stored in a retrieval system, or transmitted in any form or by any means, electronic, mechanical, photocopying, recording or otherwise, without the prior written permission of the Publisher.

First printing

Publisher Cataloging-in-Publication Data (U.S.)

Bargh, Bernard.

   Golden retriever/Bernard Bargh.

[80] p. : col. photos. ; cm.

(Dog owner's guide)

Summary: A dog owner's guide to the care and training of golden retrievers.

ISBN 1-55407-084-8

1. Golden retriever. I. Title. II. Series.

636.7527 22 SF429.G63B37 2005

Published in the United States by
Firefly Books (U.S.) Inc.
P.O. Box 1338, Ellicott Station
Buffalo, New York 14205

Printed in China

Library and Archives Canada Cataloguing in Publication

Bargh, Bernard

   Golden retriever/Bernard Bargh.
(Dog owner's guide)

ISBN 1-55407-084-8

1. Golden retriever. I. Title. II. Series.

SF429.G63B37 2005 636.752'7
C2005-900984-5

Published in Canada by
Firefly Books Ltd.
66 Leek Crescent
Richmond Hill, Ontario L4B 1H1

ACKNOWLEDGMENTS

My thanks to Mavis Chapman who has typed the manuscript, Valerie Foss for all her help and advice, and Patrick Stapleton, Deputy General Manager of the Pembroke Hotel, Blackpool, where most of this book was written. Thanks also to Gail Sherwood (Martinian) for help with photography.

CONTENTS

1 IN THE BEGINNING

The Golden Retriever was evolved by Dudley Coutts Marjoribanks, first Lord Tweedmouth (1820–1894), on his estate, Guisachan, in Scotland. The name "Golden Retriever" came later; the breed was first known as the Yellow Retriever.

It was believed that Lord Tweedmouth had seen a troupe of Russian circus dogs performing and was so taken by their intelligence that he bought the whole troupe. He then, reputedly, took the dogs to Scotland, to use on his estate, and started to breed them.

This romantic theory was disproved by a famous breeder and breed historian, Mrs. Elma Stonex. With the help of the sixth Earl of Ilchester, a relative of the first Lord Tweedmouth, it was proved that the dogs were of Scottish origin. Among information used to substantiate this claim was the stud book, kept by the first Lord Tweedmouth, which can be seen today at the Kennel Club in London, England.

This recorded that Lord Tweedmouth's first Yellow

Retriever was a single yellow pup from a litter of black, wavy-coated pups. The yellow pup was obtained from a Brighton cobbler, who had got the puppy from a gamekeeper. This puppy, called Nous, was born in June 1864, and he was the foundation sire of the breed.

Breed Ancestors

In his kennels, Lord Tweedmouth had some Tweed Water Spaniels; a breed that is now extinct. However, early writings describe these dogs as small, ordinary English Retrievers of a liver color. In those days, the term "liver" covered all the sandy colors.

One of the Tweed Water Spaniels, called Belle, was mated to Nous, and she produced four puppies. Of these, one dog, Crocus, was given to Lord Tweedmouth's eldest son; two bitches, Cowslip and Primrose,

were kept; and the other bitch, Ada, was given to Lord Tweedmouth's nephew, the fifth Earl of Ilchester, who began the Ilchester line.

Lord Tweedmouth found that a black dog mated to a yellow bitch invariably produced yellow puppies and, from the stud book, we see how he planned his litters and evolved his strain of working Retrievers from 1868 to 1890. Cowslip was mated to a Tweed Water Spaniel, and their

The first Golden Retriever was a single yellow pup from a litter of black wavy-coats.

daughter, Topsy, was mated to a black wavy-coated Retriever and produced Zoe. She, in turn, was mated to Jack, who was the result of a mating between Cowslip and Sampson, an Irish Setter.

The last two Yellow Retrievers recorded in Lord Tweedmouth's stud book were Prim and Rose, born in 1889, and they show what a skilful breeder Lord Tweedmouth was. Puppies were given to friends and relations, and they were first exhibited at a dog show in England in 1908 by Lord Harcourt, of the Culham kennels, and all his dogs went back to Lord Tweedmouth's breeding.

GROWING IN POPULARITY

Mr. McDonald, who was the head keeper to the Earl of Shrewsbury, was important in the early foundation of the breed with his Ingestre kennels. At about the same time, Mrs. W. Charlesworth started her Noranby kennels, which were the most influential in the breed for the next 40 years. In 1913, Golden Retrievers were given a separate register at the Kennel Club in London, under the name Retrievers (Golden, Yellow). The breed was recognized in Canada by the CKC in 1927, and in the United States by the AKC in 1932.

CHOOSING A GOLDEN RETRIEVER

Owning a dog will drastically alter your life for some 10 years or more, and so the first decision you have to make is whether you should own a dog at all. Remember, care and attention is necessary 365 days a year.

The next important matter to consider is your choice of dog. You may well admire the beautiful appearance of a Golden Retriever, but is the breed suited to your lifestyle? Such matters as size, coat, and breed characteristics must all be considered. The questions you must ask yourself at the outset are:

- Is my house big enough for a relatively large dog?

- Will the dog be left alone in the house for long periods while I am out at work?

- Am I active and fit enough to give a Golden the correct amount of exercise?

- Do I have the time and patience to spend grooming a long-coated breed?

- Can I afford a large dog? Vet and food bills are the chief expenses.

BREED CHARACTERISTICS

There is a song with the lines: "Beautiful to look at, delightful to behold," and so is a Golden Retriever, with his glamorous long, golden coat, which requires constant attention and grooming; as a result, the breed may not be entirely suitable for the house-proud.

The behavior patterns of your dog as a domestic pet will be strongly influenced by the work he was originally bred to do. The Golden Retriever was bred from the beginning to do a job of work in the field as a gundog,

The Golden is born to retrieve, and he will always be ready to bring you a "present."

THE KEY TO A QUIET LIFE

Being a working dog, it is imperative that your Golden gets a considerable amount of exercise; then he will be quite happy to curl up in his own quiet corner of the house, enjoying the company of his devoted owner.

retrieving shot or wounded game to his handler, hence his obsession with carrying things.

Your Golden will always want to bring "presents" to you and, in order to avoid mishaps, it is advisable to make sure your dog has plenty of toys of his own to carry around the house. In the process of bringing you a present, your Golden will never stop wagging his tail, so watch out for those valuable ornaments on low-lying tables. It's no use telling him off after he has inadvertently smashed a prized possession.

TEMPERAMENT: GENTLE GIANT

Although a comparatively large breed, most Goldens possess a gorgeous, gentle temperament, and show infinite patience with boisterous young children, coupled with a gentleness with young babies and old people.

They are blessed with extreme intelligence that is developed by human contact, hence the necessity for a single pet Golden to live in the house, where he will always be anxious to please, and will warn of any intruders.

A dog, of course, cannot speak a language but, before long, your Golden, living in the house, will seem to understand every word you utter. He will even be able to tell you the time—especially when meal times are at hand!

Goldens love cars and the very noise of keys being jangled will be a cause of great excitement; a sure sign that an outing is imminent. An open car door is viewed as an invitation to jump in.

PERFECT COMPANION

If you decide that a Golden Retriever is the right breed for you, then you will have opened up a new dimension in your life. With luck, your Golden will live to around 12 years of age, but he will remain a puppy all his life, thriving on love and attention coupled with discipline. In return, you will be repaid a thousand times by trust, affection and companionship.

THE IDEAL GOLDEN RETRIEVER

Every breed is judged by its Breed Standard, which is the written blueprint for what constitutes the "ideal dog." This is assessed in terms of general appearance, conformation, temperament and movement. Of course, there is no such thing as the perfect dog, but in the show ring it is the judge's job to find the dog that conforms as as closely as possible to the stipulations of the Breed Standard.

This has far more significance than simply finding the best-looking dog in the show ring. It is generally the show winners that are used for breeding, and so the future of the breed is at stake.

Obviously, every judge relies on their own, personal interpretation of the Standard, but there is no argument over the main characteristics that are required.

THE BREED STANDARD OF THE GOLDEN RETRIEVER

The Golden Retriever was bred to be a working gundog, and so he should be strong, powerful and balanced. His build should be symmetrical.

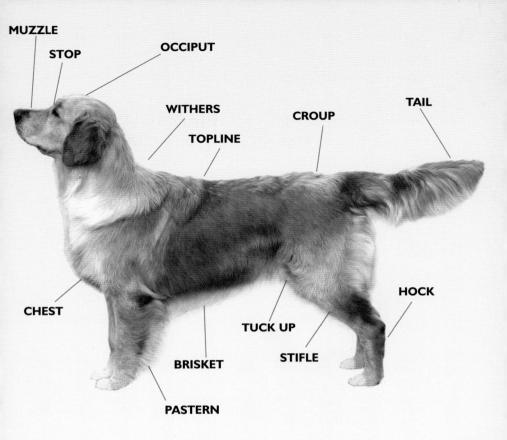

MUZZLE

STOP

OCCIPUT

WITHERS

TOPLINE

CROUP

TAIL

CHEST

TUCK UP

BRISKET

STIFLE

HOCK

PASTERN

Head

The Golden Retriever head, with its kindly, melting expression, is a hallmark of the breed, and is typical of both males and females. The skull should be broad, and the muzzle should be wide, deep and powerful. A black nose is preferred.

Eyes

The eyes should be dark in color, with dark rims. They should be set well apart and convey a friendly, intelligent expression.

The kindly, noble expression is typical of the breed.

Ears

Medium in size, and set on level with the eyes.

Mouth

The jaws should be powerful, and meet in a scissor-bite (the upper teeth closely overlapping the lower teeth).

Neck

Moderate in length, clean and muscular, gradually sloping into well-laid shoulders.

Forequarters

The shoulders should be well laid back, the forelegs straight and the elbows close-fitting.

Body

The chest is deep, and the ribs are well sprung. The topline should be level.

Hindquarters

Strong and well muscled. The stifle is well bent, and the hocks should be straight when viewed from behind.

Paws

The paws are round and catlike. The pads should be thick and hard-wearing.

Tail

The tail should be set on so that it is carried level with the back. In length, it should reach to the hocks. It should not be curled upwards.

The Golden Retriever ...
strong, powerful and balanced.

Movement

Powerful and long-striding. It should be straight and true from front and rear.

Coat

The coat can be straight or wavy. It should have good feathering, and a dense, water-resistant undercoat.

Color

All shades of cream and golden.

Red or mahogany colored dogs are faulted. In the United States, however, paler coats are considered undesirable.

Size

In the United States and Canada the height at the withers is 23–24 inches (58–60 cm) for males, and 21.5–22.5 inches (55–57 cm) for females.

Competition is intense in the breed ring.

2 BUYING A PUPPY

If you have decided that the Golden Retriever is the breed for you, it is very important that all the family should be in agreement about taking on the responsibilities of owning a dog.

They must all realize that the tasks—and some of them are just that—will have to be shared by everyone.

Obviously, the person who is most at home during the day will do the bulk of the caring, and it is better if one person is responsible for the feeding. A feeding routine, especially in puppyhood, is of great importance; this should not be trusted to a child, who is liable to forget exactly when a meal is due or, even worse, forget to feed the puppy at all!

Where To Look

When you are ready to go out and buy your puppy, the golden rule is to buy from a breeder of Golden Retrievers and not from kennels who advertise every breed under the sun.

A specialized breeder will have fed and looked after the mother (dam) correctly, and you should be able to see her, and possibly the grandmother and other close relations, when you call to see the

Take time to find a specialist breeder, with a reputation for producing sound, typical puppies.

pups. You can be confident that the pups will have been reared to the best of the breeder's ability, and you can be sure that the litter has received the right sort of food, with the required vitamins.

A breed specialist will also pay attention to the question of hereditary defects, such as hip dysplasia and cataracts (see Chapter 7). The puppies will have been regularly groomed; they will have had the correct amount of exercise for their age, and you will be charged a fair and reasonable price.

FINDING A BREEDER

How do you find a reputable breeder? All countries have a national kennel club, and they keep a list of breed clubs. Find a Golden Retriever club in your area, contact the secretary, and he or she will put you in touch with a breeder. The secretary will probably know of someone who actually has a litter of pups due.

MALE:
He is bigger
and heavier
in build.

FEMALE:
You will have
to cope with
her going
into heat.

CHOOSING BETWEEN MALE AND FEMALE

One of the most important decisions to be made at this stage is whether you wish to have a male (dog) or female (bitch). In Goldens, the dogs are just as loving as the bitches, but they are bigger and heavier.

Bitches, of course, go into heat twice a year; they always cast their coat and get a new one before actually going into heat. Looking after an in-heat bitch can be extremely difficult. The whole family needs to be on guard for the 21 days the bitch is in heat; given half a chance, she will be out looking for a mate of her choice, which could result in an unwanted litter nine weeks later.

It is often said that all bitches need one litter; this is an old wives' tale, with no foundation in fact. If you decide to have a bitch, and you are keeping her purely as a companion, you would be well advised to consult your vet as to the best time to have her neutered (spayed).

Following the operation, which is usually performed after the bitch has been in heat once, you will encounter no further problems, with the possible exception of ensuring that the bitch does not put on too much weight.

SELECTING A PUPPY

Having made the decision concerning a dog or a bitch, you are now ready to arrange a time to go to see the puppies. The breeder will probably want you to call before feeding time, as puppies soon fall asleep after they have eaten.

By this time, the puppies will be about 5 weeks old and, to you, they will all look the same. How do you pick one out, and what should you be looking for? Naturally, you will have to be guided by the breeder, but there are certain points that

you should look for:

- The puppies should be lively, alert and friendly.

- Do not fall for the pup hiding away in a corner; shyness at this stage could indicate an uncertain temperament.

- The puppies should be sturdy and nicely plump.

- Distended stomachs indicate worm infestation and, in a

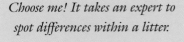

Choose me! It takes an expert to spot differences within a litter.

carefully-reared litter, deworming should have been underway for some three weeks.

- The puppies should be clean and smell nice.

- When you stroke the coat, there should be no evidence of scabs on the skin.

- There should be no discharge from the eyes and nose.

- The teeth (the ones you will see are the first teeth, which will be replaced by the second teeth at about 4 to 5 months) should be in the form of a scissor-bite, i.e., the top teeth overlap the bottom teeth.

GOLDEN COLORS

At this stage, the eye color will be grey, which gradually changes to a permanent dark brown. The nose will be jet black, although later in life some of this pigmentation is often lost. Most puppy buyers have strong views on the question of color. In most Golden Retriever litters, the colors usually vary between shades of cream and gold and, whenever possible, I let the customer have a puppy in the color of their choice. Bear in mind that the eventual color of your Golden will be the color of his ears when a puppy.

The Right Age

Puppies are ready to go to their new homes at 7 to 8 weeks. Never buy a puppy from someone who says the puppy can go earlier; you will be buying trouble. It is not natural for a puppy to be taken away from his littermates at an earlier age.

If you have picked your puppy at 5 weeks, the breeder will probably mark him with some safe vegetable dye or snip the curl from the end of his tail,

so you will know which puppy is yours when you go to collect him.

The breeder will probably ask you to call for your puppy in the morning, so that your new pride and joy will have all day to settle into strange surroundings.

Meanwhile, you now have about two weeks to make preparations for your new arrival.

The breeder will mark the pups to ensure you end up with the pup of your choice.

TIME TO GO SHOPPING

Before your puppy arrives home, there are certain preparations that should be made so that your pup gets off to a good start.

Housing
The first thing to decide is where your puppy is going to live, and what sort of bed is required. Golden Retrievers are a very loving breed, and they should be treated as such: one dog on his own must always live in the house, never in an outside kennel.

In most cases, the kitchen is deemed to be the most suitable place for your puppy to sleep.

Bed
It may be wise to start off with a crate or a cardboard box, lined with a blanket, first ensuring that any sharp metal staples have been removed.

You can then graduate to a more permanent bed, and there are many different types on the market. The plastic, kidney-

A cosy bed will be appreciated, but a crate is also a good option.

shaped beds have the advantage of being easy to clean, and they are sufficiently hard and strong, so that puppies do not find them particularly chewable.

Remember to buy a bed that is big enough for an adult Golden Retriever, and this will need to be a minimum of 36 inches (90 cm) in diameter.

Bedding

You will require two blankets or pads to fit in the bed. An absorbent fleece, which is machine-washable and can be dried very quickly, is ideal. The reason for having two pieces is so that you always have a spare when you need to wash the bedding.

Canine duvets or pet beanbags also make suitable bedding; always make sure you buy an extra cover for both types.

BOWLS

You will require two dog bowls, one for food and one for water. It is worth buying a stainless steel bowl for the food, as this type is easy to clean and will last for years. A ceramic china bowl is best for the water as, due to its weight, it cannot be easily tipped over.

23

CHOOSING A COLLAR AND LEASH

It is a good idea to fit a small, lightweight collar at a very early age. You will find that your puppy will scratch at the collar for a while, but most will soon get used to the strange sensation. I usually leave the collar on for approximately two hours, then I remove it and repeat the procedure later in the day.

Once the puppy has accepted the collar, I do not keep one on all the time. It creates a ridge around the hair, which is detrimental to showing. However, it is far more important for the well-being of the dog to ensure that you increase the size of the collar as the puppy grows. A dog must never be fitted with a collar that is too small.

At this stage, a lightweight leash can be attached. Allow the puppy to run free, with the leash attached and, eventually, you can graduate to holding the leash.

GROOMING EQUIPMENT

You will also need to buy a brush and comb, even though your puppy will require a minimum of grooming attention in the first few months. It is important that your puppy gets used to standing still while you give a quick brush, using a bristle brush.

I use a half-comb made of steel measuring 7 inches (17.5 cm) in length. There are 24 teeth on one side and 37 on the other, and I find this is ideal for teasing out the odd knot or tangle in the feathering.

All puppies can get a bit sticky after eating; you should try to sponge off the worst after meals.

TOYS

It is worth buying a few toys that can be carried and chewed by your puppy. Do not buy anything so small that it could get caught in your puppy's throat, and do not buy any toys made of rubber that could result in small pieces being chewed off.

On the subject of items being carried, remember your dog will constantly want to carry presents to you. If one of these "treasures" happens to be something you do not want the dog to have, such as a slipper or a shoe, gently take it from your puppy's mouth and replace it with one of the toys he is allowed. The idea of this is to teach the puppy to bring things to you; if you always take the item away without replacing it, you will soon get a puppy that runs off in the opposite direction.

PLAYPEN

Another item of equipment that comes in very useful is a puppy playpen. It can be used to confine the puppy in the kitchen, on the occasions when you have to go out and you do not wish to give the pup the run of the entire room. Most playpens are made of wire mesh. Ideally, it should measure 36 x 25 x 27 inches (90 x 62.5 x 67.5 cm), and it has the advantage of being easy to fold away and store when not in use.

COLLECTING YOUR PUPPY

At last, the great day arrives when it is time to collect your puppy, and your life will never be the same again. For the next six months, your puppy will need attention morning, noon and, hopefully, not too much at night.

I have always found the best way to collect a puppy is for someone else to drive the car, and to have the puppy on my lap (which is covered with a thick towel). Make sure you have some newspapers and paper towels within easy reach.

Some puppies are never carsick; they just curl up on your lap and go to sleep, but it is a good idea to be prepared. Most sensible

breeders do not feed a puppy before the journey, so minimizing the chance of such accidents. If you have to travel alone, the puppy playpen or crate can be put to good use.

THE PAPERWORK

When you collect your puppy, the breeder should give you a folder containing some important documents. Make sure you receive a vaccination certificate (if the puppy has received his first shots), records of deworming, tattooing or microchipping and transfer of ownership (if applicable). In the United States, the breeder obtains a "Blue Slip" for each purebred puppy from the American Kennel Club (AKC); the new owner then sends it to the AKC in return for a full registration certificate.

In Canada, the breeder receives a registration certificate from the Canadian Kennel Club (CKC) which is then forwarded to the new owner.

The breeder should provide you with a copy of your puppy's pedigree. Most pedigree forms allow space for five generations. The top half concerns the breeding of the sire (father), and the bottom half relates to the dam (mother). Champions are written or underlined in red.

3 HOME AT LAST

The first night can be a traumatic time for both puppy and owner. The puppy will feel very lost, spending the first night away from the warmth and comfort of littermates, and you should do your best to help him settle easily.

Many people have their own ideas on the best way of doing this, but I think that warmth is an essential ingredient. If your puppy has been fed, and you make sure the bed is warm, possibly providing a toy for the pup to snuggle up to, hopefully sleep will win the day!

FINDING A VET

Like a good doctor, a good vet is worth his or her weight in gold, and it is worth talking to dog-owning friends in your neighborhood, who will probably recommend a practice.

HOUSEBREAKING

If done properly, this will take more of your time during the first few weeks than any other task. The secret is that, the moment your puppy wakes up or finishes a meal, you take him outside immediately and give him lots of praise when he does the necessary. It is no use putting the pup out alone; you must go out too, come hail, rain or snow.

Do not chastise your pup for the odd "mistake" in the house. At this very young age, a pup has no real control over his bodily functions, and it is really your fault for not anticipating your pup's needs.

At night, place a newspaper on the floor by the door (or in an area of his playpen or crate), and you will be amazed at how quickly your puppy gets the message. Don't forget to praise your pup in the morning if the newspaper has been used.

One final tip: make an effort to get up earlier than usual, and you might even beat your pup to it.

If you take your pup out at regular intervals, he will soon understand what is required.

FIRST VACCINATIONS

Puppies are routinely vaccinated against distemper, hepatitis, parvovirus and parainfluenza. Vaccinating against leptospurosis also recommended in areas where the disease is endemic. Vaccination against rabies is compulsory in Canada and parts of the United States. You should not take your puppy outside your own house and yard until two weeks after the final shot, and you should not allow the pup to come into contact with other dogs during that time.

Different vets use different products, and this affects the start date of the vaccination program and the interval between shots.

My vet vaccinates at 8 or 10 weeks, followed by a second shot at 12 weeks. This means that the earliest the puppy can go out into the big, wide world is at 14 weeks. It is wise to start socialization immediately after

Your vet will advise you when to vaccinate your puppy.

this period of isolation, so that your puppy gets used to all sorts of different experiences. This will aid your dog's mental development and prevent problems later in life.

DEWORMING

Your puppy should have been dewormed by the time you take charge. Ask the breeder for details of any treatments given, and then discuss the matter with your vet. He or she will recommend a suitable brand, and advise you on dosage.

BEWARE OF OVERDOING IT

For the first four months, do not overexercise your puppy. The muscles are not developed and too much exercise can hamper development.

The puppy will get all the exercise he needs by running free around the yard, plus very short walks when the socialization period begins.

IDENTITY TAG

When you start to take your puppy out for regular exercise, make sure you attach an identity tag to his collar showing the dog's name, along with your name, address and telephone number. The collar should be made of soft, rolled leather.

SLEEP

A puppy requires plenty of peaceful, uninterrupted sleep; as much as a human baby, in fact. It is vital to remember that a puppy is not a plaything, and children must not be allowed to disturb the puppy when he wants to sleep. A tired puppy soon becomes irritable, and you could be creating future problems if you do not allow your puppy to have adequate rest periods.

Watch the signs; your pup will tell you when he is ready for a rest.

FEEDING YOUR GOLDEN RETRIEVER

A healthy, balanced diet is essential for the well-being of your Golden Retriever but, nowadays, there are so many types of dog food and methods of feeding that it can be quite baffling for the new owner to decide on the best diet to use. There are basically three different methods of feeding your dog:

Complete Feeds

These usually come in some pellet form and, as the name implies, they are "complete," containing everything your dog needs. They are nutritionally balanced and include all the vitamins and other additives your dog requires.

In most cases, there are different complete diets available to meet particular requirements, such as puppy growth, adult maintenance, working dogs and nursing bitches.

The diet can be fed dry or soaked. If it is fed dry, it is essential to make sure that plenty of fresh water is available at all times.

Orthodox Methods

This involves canned meat or unrefined tripe, plus soaked kibble, with various additives. The quality of canned food varies, and the owner would be well advised to examine the breakdown of contents closely (listed on the label), before deciding on which brand to feed.

Natural Diet

Meat, fed raw, and kibble. With this method, meat and kibble are not fed together.

The kibble is always wholemeal, and vegetables and herbs complete the diet. Care must be taken that all the necessary vitamins and minerals are included. Ask your vet for advice.

CHOOSING A DIET

For the first few days, keep to the diet the breeder has been feeding; this will help to minimize the puppy's trauma of moving to new surroundings.

Every dog owner finds the method of feeding that is most convenient for their particular lifestyle, and the type of food that suits the individual dog. However, there are some useful tips, which are worth bearing in mind:

- Dogs are creatures of habit, and regular mealtimes are a must.

- Never leave food down indefinitely; if it is not eaten within ten minutes, it should be thrown away.

- Always serve food at room temperature, never straight from the refrigerator.

8 WEEKS OLD

At this age, a puppy should be eating three or four meals daily. Feed him a good quality kibble (growth formula) served dry, or moistened according to the breeder's instructions.

Some breeders recommend feeding a raw diet. If this is the plan you choose to follow, ask the breeder for a complete diet sheet. This is more complicated than the all-in-one kibbles available since you will have to ensure your puppy receives all the nutrients necessary for his growth. Supplements such as yogurt, cottage cheese or cooked minced beef can be added (ask the breeder or your vet for guidelines).

TIPS ON FEEDING

- Give your puppy a dog biscuit at bedtime, and always leave a supply of fresh, clean water available.

- Ask your vet's advice when choosing a kibble to feed your dog. Vets' offices frequently stock high-quality food that is not offered in grocery stores or pet supply stores.

- Between 3 and 6 months, puppies are fed three meals a day.

- From 6 months on, dogs should receive two meals a day. Even as an adult this practice should be continued — dividing the daily ration into a morning and evening feed — because it is easier on the digestive system.

- Between 9 and 12 months, the kibble should be changed from a growth formula to a maintenance formula.

- If your dog is very active, a high-performance kibble might be necessary. This should be easy to judge; keep an eye on your dog's weight and appetite and adjust the kind of kibble and amount fed accordingly.

A puppy has a tremendous rate of growth between 3 and 12 months.

4 EARLY LEARNING

A puppy officially becomes a young adult or a teenager when he reaches the age of 12 months.

At this age, serious obedience and gundog training can begin (see Chapter 6); until then, there is a lot of preparatory work to be done, without boring your young puppy.

I always believe in letting a Golden enjoy his puppy days, and any training I do is always on the basis of "little and often."

One of the first things your puppy must learn is his name. By using it as a preface to all instructions, or when putting down his food, you will be amazed at how quickly he gets the message.

The Golden puppy is eager to learn.

CANINE COMMUNICATION

One of the most important things to learn when training is that a dog does not understand English. I once saw an owner shouting the command "Sit" to a puppy who had not the slightest idea what he was talking about. I pointed out to the embarrassed gentleman that if, at the same time he gave the command, he gently pressed down on the dog's back-end, all would be well, and it was.

TRAINING EXERCISES

Teaching the Sit

- Show your puppy a treat, and then hold it above his head so that he has to lift up his head and lower his rear to reach it.

- As soon as he sits, say "Sit" and give him the treat and lots of praise.

- Practice little and often, until the dog will sit whenever you

Don't allow your puppy to jump up at visitors. This should be stopped from the outset by the command "No," coupled with the action of putting the dog's feet back on the ground and then ignoring him. Dogs jump up to get attention; by ignoring him, your Golden will soon learn that his efforts don't work.

Reward your pup as soon as he goes into the Sit position.

ask, without you having to lure him into position.

● Use the exercise in your everyday routine, such as before giving the puppy a meal or when putting his leash on before a walk. He will then associate being obedient with rewarding experiences.

Teaching the Down

● This is taught in a similar way to the Sit exercise.

● Show your puppy a treat, and then lower your hand to the ground so the puppy has to lower his body to reach it.

● As soon as his tummy hits the floor, say "Down" and give him the treat. Remember to praise him profusely so as to encourage him.

● Again, practice little and often, and your Golden will soon be lying down quicker and quicker each time.

Teaching the Stay

● To teach your Golden to stay, sit him off the leash. If you are practicing in your yard, face away from home. The reason

Start with your puppy in the Sit and use a treat to lure him into the Down.

for this is that, when you step back, the dog will be less likely to move towards you than if he thought you were backing away towards home.

● Back off about 4 yards (3.5 m), with your right hand raised, saying "Sit."

● Then return and praise the dog.

● Repeat, backing off a bit further, again return and praise.

TEACHING YOUR PUP TO COME WHEN CALLED

- As soon as you consider your puppy is steady enough in the Sit position, and you can retreat without the dog moving, you can now try calling your dog to you.

- The procedure is to have your dog sit, again facing away from home.

- Now, back away about 20 yards (18 m) with your hand raised, repeating occasionally the command "Sit."

- Walk all the way back to your dog,

praise, and repeat the procedure a second time.

- Walk away for a third time, stop, face the dog, and call him to you, using his name. With luck, the dog will come bounding up to you.

- Soon, you can introduce three short blasts on the whistle, as well as calling by name.

- Finally, repeat a fourth time and, (without calling his name), walk back to the dog.

Wait until he is steady in the Sit before attempting a formal recall.

NOW CALL HIS NAME

You will notice that you have called your dog to you only once in four exercises, so alleviating the danger of the dog anticipating your call. In this exercise, you used the dog's name for the first time; we saved up this little treat until the moment you wanted the dog to run at speed towards you. After about two weeks (14 half-hour sessions), you should have a young dog who will sit, stay and come to you on verbal or whistle command. Remember, each dog is an individual, and some may take longer to get the message than others. A training class will help you to master all aspects of training.

LEASH-TRAINING

Hopefully, during the 8- to 14-week isolation period, you will have got the puppy used to wearing a small, lightweight collar with a leash attached.

● With the dog on your left-hand side, take a couple of steps forward, and encourage your dog to walk with you.

● Say "Heel" and praise and reward him only when he is walking alongside you.

● If he pulls forward, stop still.

● Call him back to you, sit him on your left-hand side, and start again.

● Over frequent, short practice sessions, increase the number of steps you walk forward, vary your pace, and introduce turns.

● Dogs pull on the leash because they want to get somewhere quickly. If you stop every time the leash becomes taut, your dog will realize that pulling is fruitless.

Sometimes, a young dog develops a nasty habit of pulling away and sideways from you. This problem can be solved quite easily by walking along the side of a wall, so that the dog cannot pull away leftward because of the wall, and cannot pull to the right because you are there.

Encourage your pup to follow you when he is on the leash.

MAKE SURE IT IS FUN

Keep training sessions short, and break them up with play. Reward your puppy with verbal praise, stroking and treats. A puppy has a short concentration span, and it is important not to tax him too much. The aim is to make training fun, and then you will find that your puppy really looks forward to his lessons.

OUT IN THE BIG, WIDE WORLD

By the time your puppy is 14 weeks old, his vaccinations will have taken effect (see Chapter 3), and it will be time to introduce him to the big, wide world.

For the first trip outside your home and yard, providing your puppy is reasonably proficient on the leash, go for a short ride in the car (but not immediately after a meal). Then find a quiet spot where you can let the pup out for a very short walk on the leash.

Hopefully, your pup will meet one or two friendly dogs, as the last thing you want is for the puppy to be upset by a bad-tempered dog on his first outing.

The final trick is to get your puppy home without being carsick. Do not be disheartened if the pup is sick within 50 yards (46 m) of arriving home; it often happens. Very soon, your puppy will be so used to the car that it is a job to keep him out of it.

You will also want to accustom your puppy to car rides so that he has a chance to run free. I always pick a spacious area that is safe with regard to traffic, for one of

When your pup has completed his vaccinations, he is ready to venture out into the big, wide world.

the problems you will probably encounter is that the puppy will not come to you while running free. If you have another dog in the house, take him with you so that when the older dog comes to you, the puppy will more than likely follow.

Golden Rules

Two golden rules on this subject are:

● Never run after the puppy. The secret is to run away from the pup, preferably towards the parked car and, more often than not, your puppy will come running after you, afraid of being left. If you have bought yourself a whistle, you can call and whistle while running away. Three short blasts repeated regularly, mean "come back to me at once." If this is practiced often enough, the puppy will soon return to you on hearing the whistle alone.

● Never chastise your puppy when he eventually returns to you or, very soon, he will relate coming to you with a telling off. The opposite should be practiced, lots of praise and lots of fussing.

Always make a big fuss of your puppy when he comes back to you.

5

CARING FOR YOUR GOLDEN

When you are caring for a living creature, human or canine, it is essential to get into good habits so that you establish a balanced routine for you and your dog.

There is no point in being too ambitious in your plans: you must work out the routine of care (and fun) that will suit your lifestyle.

CHOOSING
THE RIGHT AMOUNT OF EXERCISE

I have eight Goldens, each requiring different amounts of exercise, so they are usually taken out in three lots, but never more than four at a time. When deciding on the "teams," I take several factors into account. The older dogs do not, obviously, require as much exercise

as a 3-year-old, and a young 9-month-old puppy also needs limited exercise. I often find it is a good idea to take a couple of the old dogs with a young puppy, as they all require roughly the same amount of exercise, and the experience of the old ones soon rubs off on the youngsters.

DAILY ROUTINE

For my dogs, morning exercise usually entails a trip in the car to the sand dunes (sometimes the beach), and consists of free running along the dunes for one mile (1.6 km), and free running along the promenade (hard surface) on our return to the car: a round trip of approximately two miles (3.2 km).

Back at home, the dogs go into the kennels, which have covered runs and outside runs, both surfaces being made of concrete. The kennel floors are covered with sawdust and/or wood shavings, which are marvelous

The adult Golden thrives on exercise.

if the dogs have got dirty or wet while out on exercise. If, however, the dogs have been exercised in pouring rain, they are always dried with a chamois leather (very good for soaking up the wet) and toweled before being put in the kennels.

The dogs do not normally sleep in the kennels. Goldens are housedogs first and foremost. We always make sure there is a constant supply of cold water available. In the summer it is changed at regular intervals.

The dogs are also taken out later in the day, and for a short break before bed, giving them a chance to relieve themselves.

TAKE IT EASY

In a puppy's early formative days, it is absolutely essential not to overexercise. No long, tiring walk, either on or off the leash; again, "little and often" with plenty of rest and sleep in between. Apart from socializing youngsters and accustoming them to the outside world, my puppies do not go off the premises until they are 6 months old.

FEEDING THE ADULT GOLDEN

After exercising the dogs, I make the food for the day, which consists of soaked 100 percent wheatmeal kibble, plus meat. The amounts vary for each dog but, as a guide, an active young adult gets 0.5 lb (227 g) kibble plus 1 lb (454 g) of meat. If I feed kibble and meat together, I always soak the kibble for one hour in hot water (with yeast extract added), before adding the meat. This is because I prefer the swelling of the kibble to take place before entering the dog's stomach.

If you wish to feed hard kibble, give them at lunchtime. Feed meat on its own in the evening, which can be in the form of canned meat, canned tripe or raw, black tripe available from firms that specialize in this type of product.

When the preparation of the dog's meal is completed, I add one garlic tablet (nature's antiseptic), ten yeast tablets (during winter months), and two tea-spoonfuls of seaweed powder (for coat and pigmentation). The dogs receive one-third of the total meal pre-pared at around midday, and the rest at about 6 p.m.

Of course, there are other methods of feeding, such as the complete foods (see page 33). These contain everything a dog needs, and are much easier to feed, as they need no preparation. However, I think that complete foods, although very nutritious, must become very boring and uninteresting for the dog.

A complete diet will take care of all your dog's nutritional needs.

CHEWING THINGS OVER …

At about 4 to 5 months, a puppy will cut his new teeth, so unless you want the furniture ruined, make sure your puppy has plenty of things to chew. When all the new teeth have arrived, check that none of the old ones are left (particularly the puppy canine teeth). If you have any doubts, let the vet have a look.

GROOMING YOUR GOLDEN

Before the lunchtime feed, all my dogs are groomed and, while this is being done, a daily inspection is carried out for possible ear or skin problems. Most Goldens cannot wait for their turn to be groomed; they usually lie down while they are being groomed, which presents an ideal opportunity for a general check.

Puppy Care

A puppy coat does not need a lot of attention, but it is important that your Golden gets used to being groomed from an early age. The adult Golden has a lot of feathering and will need regular grooming sessions. This is much easier for both dog and handler if your dog is used to the routine.

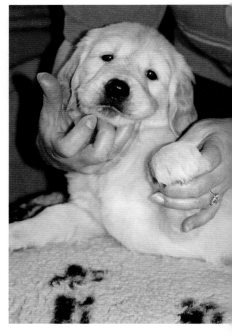

To start with, get your puppy accustomed to being handled all over. Stroke him from head to tail, roll him over and tickle him on his tummy. Lift his ears and look inside, and gently open his mouth to inspect his teeth. Give your pup lots of praise when he cooperates, and when you have finished, reward him with a treat or have a game with a favorite toy. If you meet any resistance, be firm and give plenty of encouragement. As soon as your pup does as he is asked, reward him.

You can now move on to using a bristle brush. To begin with, just give a few strokes with the brush, and reward him. It is also a good idea to get your pup used to the feel of a comb going through his coat.

You may find it easier to place your pup on a table for his grooming sessions. He will need to be carefully supervised, but most pups quickly learn that they must not jump off the table. It makes the task of grooming a lot less backbreaking.

Adult Care

The adult Golden will need regular grooming, using both a brush and a comb. Start by brushing through the coat, methodically working from the head down to the chest, along the body to the hindquarters and then the tail. It will be easier if your Golden lies on his side so that you can get to his undercarriage.

It is the feathering that needs particular attention as this can mat and tangle very easily. The legs, tail and undercarriage will need to be combed through. The worst place for mats forming is behind the ears, so make sure you always check this area.

Grooming provides an ideal opportunity to check your dog over.

ROUTINE CHECKS

Ears

Check the ears to make sure they are clean and smell fresh. You can clean external dirt with damp cotton wool, but do not try to probe into the ear canal: you could end up doing more harm than good. If the ear is red and inflamed, or appears to be dirty and foul-smelling, seek veterinary advice.

Eyes

The eyes should be bright and sparkling, with no evidence of redness or inflammation. You can clean away debris with damp cotton wool, but if your dog has a continual discharge from the eyes, you should consult your vet.

Teeth

Chewing bones helps to keep teeth clean, but dogs that are fed on a soft, complete diet often need extra help to keep their teeth clean.

It is a good idea to get into the habit of giving your Golden's teeth a weekly brush, and this will keep the teeth free from tartar, and the gums free from infection.

You can buy a toothbrush and toothpaste especially for dogs and, if you get your dog used to the routine, he will not object.

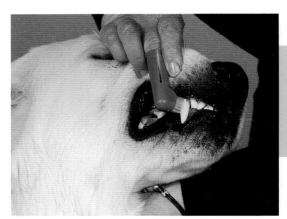

Regular brushing will keep the teeth and gums healthy.

CARING FOR PAWS AND NAILS

Check the pads to make sure there are no cracks or cuts.

This should be done every time you return from a walk, as well as at your regular grooming sessions.

If you exercise your Golden on hard surfaces, his nails will wear down naturally, but if this is not the case, you will need to trim them.

You can buy nail clippers, which are easy to operate, but it is advisable to ask your vet to show you what to do in the first instance.

There is a quick in the nail, and if you cut into it, it will bleed profusely.

BATHING YOUR GOLDEN RETRIEVER

On the question of bathing, my dogs get bathed once a year, preferably in the yard on a lovely, hot summer's afternoon. If you have to bath your dog in the winter, it is better to use the bathroom and put the dog in the bath, using a shower appliance to wet the dog. Bathing is a two-handed job, and one dog per day is quite enough for anyone.

● First of all, the dog is soaked to the skin with warm water.

● Then a proprietary dog shampoo is applied and worked into a rich lather.

● The suds should be completely rinsed off before applying a dog shampoo conditioner, which should be left on the dog for about three minutes.

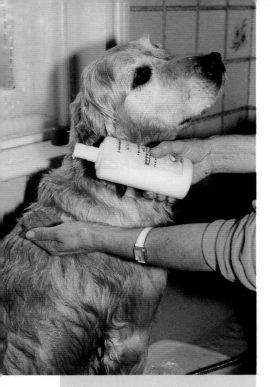

There are times when your Golden needs a freshen-up.

- Now is the time to rinse, rinse and rinse again with clean, warm water, making sure all the conditioner and any of the original shampoo is out of the coat.

- On a summer's day, let the dog run around the yard, shaking himself, and then get to work drying him with a chamois leather and warm towels.

- Let the sun do the rest while you continue to brush and comb the coat in the direction required.

- If you are bathing indoors, a hairdryer is invaluable; but make sure it is not too hot for your dog.

SOME USEFUL DO'S AND DON'TS

- DO be a responsible owner and pick up after your dog in public places.

- DO get your dog used to having his paws wiped before coming into the house.

- DO put your dog on his collar and leash before opening the car door.

- DO take the trouble to exercise your dog at least twice every day.

- DON'T let your dog out of the house so that he can run wild in the street.

- DON'T let your dog out in the yard and expect him to exercise himself; he won't.

THE VETERAN GOLDEN

It is important to remember that, as he reaches old age, your Golden will need special care.

- Keep your dog warm (old dogs often suffer from rheumatism).
- Watch your dog's weight (an old, fat dog is not a happy one).
- Feed two meals instead of one large meal (the dog's digestive system will have deteriorated).
- Do not overexercise.
- Do not neglect trimming and bathing just because old age is approaching.
- Six-month routine vet check-ups are advisable, to catch any early signs of illness.

THE FINAL GOODBYE

The wheel has almost gone full circle, and the dreaded decision of when to part with your old, ailing dog is at hand. Remember: it is the interests of the dog that are of paramount importance, and a delay can cause much unnecessary suffering. Be guided by your vet and, when the moment arrives for him to give the shot, pluck up the courage to be present so that your dog can die in your arms, hearing your voice. I always have my dogs cremated, and I insist that I receive the correct ashes so that they can be buried in my yard.

6 THE VERSATILE RETRIEVER

The Golden Retriever is a versatile breed that excels in many sports and occupations. Quick to learn and eager to please, he is a joy to train and work with.

The Gundog

A Golden Retriever is a gundog; and his job in the field, as his name implies, is to find and retrieve shot and wounded game tenderly to hand.

If, when you decide to buy a Golden Retriever puppy, your prime aim is for him to be used as a shooting dog, it is wise to purchase from a working strain. Working lines are more biddable and trainable because that is what they are bred for. They are, however, much more wiry in appearance than Goldens that are bred for the show ring.

If you buy from a show breeder, there is no need to worry: all Golden Retrievers have the instinct to carry and retrieve, as you will notice and, hopefully, encourage, while your puppy grows up.

It is not possible, in the space of this chapter to go into the details of Field Trials and Working Tests. I will outline the basic principles of simple retrieving. If you then wish to proceed further, you should consult an advanced book on the subject.

IMPORTANT LESSONS FOR THE OWNER

"It's the owner who needs training, not the dog." So said John Halstead, the famous gundog trainer. John's training classes, which I attended for some two years, were full of blunt, down-to-earth common sense. The basic rules included:

● Train little and often; half an hour, once or twice a day.

● Patience is a virtue; do not take the dog out if you are in a bad mood.

● Your tone of voice is all-important.

● Remember, each dog has a different character; some need coaxing, others firm handling.

● Get the dog to concentrate on you; if he is doing that, he won't be thinking about anything else.

● Choose a completely quiet place for early training; the last thing you need is children or other distractions appearing at the vital moment.

● Always stop on a high note; you will be happy and the dog most certainly will be.

Goldens bred from working lines tend to be more trainable.

OBEDIENCE IS ALL

Before any retrieving is attempted, your puppy or young adult must be 100 percent obedient to Sit, Stay, and Come commands (see pages 37–40). When your dog is sent out for that first retrieve, it is imperative that he returns to you with his prize, and does not run off to the other end of the field imagining that it is some sort of game.

TEACHING THE RETRIEVE

Once the obedience training has been perfected, teaching the actual retrieving is comparatively easy; after all, that is what a Golden has been bred for.

- Start the retrieving practice in a restricted area, just in case the puppy decides to forget all he has previously learned. The ground I use for the first few lessons is 100 yards (90 m) long, with gates at each end, and 10 yards (9 m) wide, with a hedge on either side.

- For the first retrieve, use a small, lightweight, green canvas dummy (purchased from any good gun shop).

- Repeat exactly the same procedure adopted when teaching the dog to stay, i.e.,

Start by getting your pup focussed on a toy.

sit the dog off the leash facing away from home, back off about four yards (3.5 m) with your right hand raised, saying "Sit."

- You are now facing the dog, standing four yards in front, with your hand up telling the dog to sit.

- Now, out of your pocket, produce the dummy and throw it backwards over your shoulder, at the same time making sure the dog does not move.

- Return to the dog, wait for a few seconds, and then send the dog for the dummy.

- The moment the dog's head goes down to retrieve, shout his name and use your whistle to encourage the dog to return.

- Then, gently take the dummy from the dog's mouth, saying "Dead," and give much praise.

- Assuming the first retrieve was successful, call it a day and finish on a high note for both you and your dog.

Throw the toy and encourage your pup to bring it back to you.

Encouraging

You will have noticed that we threw the dummy away from home, the idea being that, when the dog returned with the dummy, he was going towards home, so encouraging him to

return to you. Next, stand by the dog's side instead of in front, move out of the restricted area and, in time, longer and longer retrieves will be possible.

GAME RETRIEVES

After a few weeks with the canvas dummy, progress to using a bird dummy, which is slightly bigger and heavier.

Once the dog is comfortable with the larger dummy, let him retrieve a hen pheasant. If the dog is not too keen to pick it up, I go back to the canvas dummy, with the wings of the pheasant wrapped around it. Once the dog retrieves that, go back to a new hen pheasant, and there should not be any further problems.

You will have noticed, so far, we have been using cold game and, usually, it is but a short step to the dog becoming proficient at retrieving newly shot game.

Basspro Shops (basspro.com) have extensive catalogs of sports equipment including equipment for training a retriever with birds. For actual training, contact your breed club or local hunting retriever club; or speak to your vet who may well be able to advise you on local clubs.

The next step is retrieving a bird dummy. Goldens rarely have a problem with this.

GETTING USED TO GUNFIRE

A Retriever should regard the sound of a shot as of no consequence whatsoever; it must never become a signal for a dash out to retrieve, neither should a dog be gun-shy. However, in the early days of training, quite a few dogs are "gun-nervous," and there is a vast difference between the two. Providing a puppy gets used to distant bangs and loud noises from 5 weeks of age, when his hearing becomes acute, you rarely encounter any problems. As the puppy is growing up, I often fire my starting pistol, equipped with blanks, while the pup is feeding: first at a distance, and then getting closer as the dog gets older. At a later date, I change to my 12-gauge, again fired at an ever-decreasing distance.

COMPETITIVE OBEDIENCE

The obedience taught to your puppy, in conjunction with his retrieving, will be of great help if you decide to go in for Competitive Obedience. There are many training clubs to choose from, and Goldens have proved that they excel in this field.

The exercises in Competitive Obedience become progressively more difficult as you move up the ranks. The ultimate aim is for your dog to become an Obedience Champion.

There are minor differences in the exercises depending on where you are competing. For example, the United States has an Agility section incorporated into their competitions, but the other exercises are on similar lines to the UK format.

HEELWORK: Dog and handler must perform Heelwork on and off the leash, at different paces, and including left turns, right turns and about turns.

STAYS: The dog must stay in the Sit, Stand or Down for an allocated length of time. In the more advanced classes, handlers must be out of sight.

RECALLS: The dog must be commanded to Wait, and then recalled to the handler, who is either standing still or on the move. If the handler is standing still, the dog must go into the Present position, and then Finish ending up on the handler's left-hand side. If the handler is on the move, the dog must come into the Heel position, and move off with the handler.

SENDAWAY: The judge marks out a square box, and the handler must send the dog to the designated area where he should go into an instant Down.

RETRIEVE: The retrieve article may be a dumbbell or a glove.

  The dog must go to Fetch on command, pick up the article cleanly, and then present it to the handler.

DISTANT CONTROL: The handler stands at a distance from the dog, and when commanded, the dog must go into the Sit, Stand, or Down.

Dumbbell Retrieve: control and precision are vital ingredients for this exercise.

SCENT DISCRIMINATION: A number of scent cloths (usually around 10) are set out in the ring. The dog must find a scent cloth with the handler's scent, pick it up and return with it to the handler. In more advanced classes, the dog must find an article with the judge's scent, and decoys may also be used. This test is done at advanced levels.

AGILITY

Agility is now immensely popular and is taught and practiced at most training clubs. It is gratifying to note that Golden Retrievers are reaching the highest level in this sphere.

AGE CONCERN

Jumping on and off obstacles, and clearing hurdle and tire jumps can put considerable strain on your dog's joints. For this reason, Agility training is not permitted until a dog is 12 months old.

Agility is a fun obstacle course for dogs, with the dog having to negotiate a series of obstacles, competing against the clock. Faults can be incurred for knocking a pole down, taking the wrong route and missing the painted area on contact equipment. It is a fast sport, which demands control and accuracy as well as speed. The equipment used for Agility competitions includes the following obstacles:

Hurdles

The height may vary depending on the dog's height category and the organizing body, but usually they are 2 feet 6 inches (75 cm).

Dog Walk

The dog must run up the ascending plank, touching the contact area, along the horizontal plank and down the descending plank, again touching the contact area.

A-Frame

This involves a fast run to get up the frame and then over the top. There are contact areas getting on and off.

Tunnels

These can be rigid or collapsible. The dog must run through them at speed.

Tire

This can be set in a frame, or made into a lollipop.

Pause Table

The dog must jump on the table and stay in the Down or Sit position for the required length of time.

Seesaw

This is another piece of contact equipment, so the dog must step on and off the seesaw without missing the marked area.

Weave Poles

A series of poles that the dog must learn to weave through.

The athletic Golden makes an excellent Agility competitor.

ASSISTANCE DOGS

The Golden Retriever is an intelligent dog, and is eager to please. For this reason, the breed has been selected for some of the most important service tasks.

Guide Dogs

Golden Retrievers are used throughout the world as guide dogs for the blind. They are the right height for guiding, and they are calm and steady despite all the distractions of a busy environment.

Hearing Dogs

This is a relatively new area for Goldens, but again the breed has proved to be highly successful. In this work, the more sensitive side of the Golden's temperament comes to the fore.

Dogs for the Disabled

Dogs who work with disabled people must be able to accomplish a wide variety of tasks so that they can help their owners in all aspects of everyday life. This includes getting the laundry out of the washing machine, opening doors, fetching items, and picking up dropped objects. The dog must also walk calmly alongside a wheelchair, and be calm in every situation he is likely to encounter.

Sniffer Dogs

Golden Retrievers are in great demand as sniffer dogs, detecting drugs and explosives. This is where the breed's tremendous sense of smell comes into play, as well as having the ability to work on their own initiative.

Therapy Dogs

Therapy dogs visit people in hospitals and homes for the elderly, and some also go into schools. This is immensely valuable work, and the sweet, kindly nature of the Golden makes him an ideal choice.

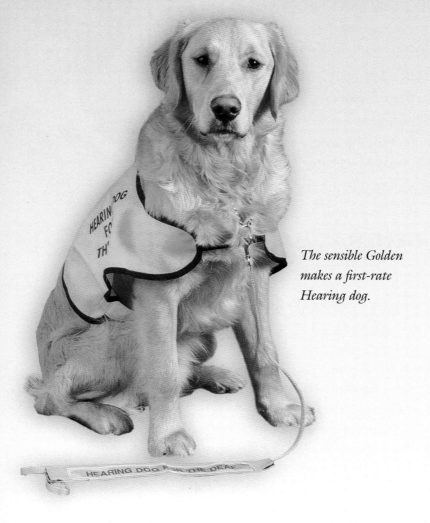

The sensible Golden makes a first-rate Hearing dog.

7 HEALTH CARE

The Golden is a hardy breed and, with common sense and attention to detail, visits to the vet can be reduced or kept to a minimum. Working on the basis that prevention is better than cure, the following tips are essential for the wellbeing of your Golden Retriever.

GENERAL MAINTENANCE

ECTOPARASITES

Ectoparasites include fleas, lice, ticks and mange. They live in or on the skin of your dog and, just as a child with the best home conditions can get lice, so your dog can acquire these parasites.

Fleas

These cause itching, and in some dogs, flea bites can cause intense irritation. In bad cases, you can see thin, elongated, brown wingless insects with long legs running over the skin and jumping off the animal. They can be found all over the body, but are usually particularly evident around the neck and head, and at the base of the tail. Flea droppings, which are often left in the dog's coat, are black, hard, and the size of grains of sand.

The new spot-on treatments (usually applied once a month) are quick and easy to use. They are effective at all stages of the flea's development.

Lice

These feed on the skin and lay eggs on the hair. They may be prevalent around the dog's neck and ears, and the inside of the thighs. They are light-brown, fat and wingless, and must be treated with a prescribed insecticide. The treatment is usually repeated at a later stage in order to kill the newly-hatched lice. Your vet will recommend a product and give application instructions.

Routine treatment is needed to prevent the infestation of fleas.

Ticks

These brownish-white, rounded insects, the size of a pea or a bean, are usually caught when the dog goes through areas where sheep or deer have been.

Ticks feed by sucking blood from the dog. They are usually found on the head, neck and shoulders, during the summer months.

A tick attaches itself to the dog by its mouthpiece, and care must be taken that you do not leave the tick's head embedded in the dog's skin when you try to remove it, as this can cause severe skin infection.

These parasites can be removed by using cotton wool, well dampened with hydrogen peroxide. If this is held in position covering the tick for approximately five minutes, the tick will loosen its hold.

Lyme disease (transmitted by deer ticks) is a serious disease in both dogs and humans, and preventive measures should be taken.

Mange

There are two common types: sarcoptic or follicular. Mange causes intense irritation, which can result in the dog scratching until blood appears on the affected area. Susceptible areas are generally around the head, the neck, the ears, under the body,

and the inside of the thighs and fore legs.

Sarcoptic mange is readily transmissible from dog to dog, so it is essential that all dogs living in the same area are treated. Your vet will advise on the most suitable brand of insecticidal shampoo to use. With all skin complaints, including eczema, the sooner you start veterinary treatment, the better.

It is, however, of great importance that you provide your vet with as much information as possible.

This includes such matters as the type of fluids used to clean the kitchen floor and carpets, and the brand of aerosol sprays that are used in the house.

This may seem irrelevant, but your dog may be allergic to one of these products, and the treatment prescribed by your vet could be seriously undermined.

WORMS

Puppies should be dewormed four roundworms, before and after they leave the breeder. Tapeworms, whipworms and hookworms are also common problems. Heartworm can be fatal to dogs and is endemic in parts of the United States and Canada; ask your vet to test your dog and recommend an appropriate preventive treatment.

Your Golden's health depends on regular deworming.

EXERCISE IS THE KEY

A Golden requires free-running exercise every day; it is no use restricting your dog all week and then going on a marathon at the weekend. Sensible exercise, combined with a balanced diet, should guarantee ideal body weight.

Grooming

My dogs are groomed every day, but once or twice a week should suffice for the pet owner. Take the opportunity to inspect for anything that may be amiss, such as running eyes, wax in the ears, growths, or cut pads.

Vaccinations

Your puppy will have had his initial shots in the first few months of his life (see Chapter 2) but, he will need booster shots at regular intervals for the rest of his life. Ask your vet for more details.

Your vet will help you to plan initial vaccinations and subsequent boosters.

SIGNS TO WATCH OUT FOR

Motions

A dog's motions are a good indicator of his general state of health. If you detect any looseness, it is a sign of a possible problem. Quite often, the trouble is caused by diet, and this can easily be adjusted by feeding rice and white meat or fish, plus a treatment from your vet to settle the stomach.

If the condition persists and turns to diarrhea, the problem may be an infection of some description, and you should seek further advice from your vet.

If you are worried about your dog's eating habits, consult your vet.

Refusal of Food

If your dog is reluctant to eat, never try to force-feed. If the condition persists, it is a sign that all is not well, and you should contact your vet.

Sickness and Vomiting

The golden rule in this situation is that, whenever a dog is sick, never administer anything by the mouth: no food, no liquid, no medicine. Starve your dog for 12 to 24 hours. You can let the dog lick ice cubes to prevent dehydration.

If no further sickness has occurred, introduce a diet of white meat or fish plus boiled rice, the secret being "a little, often." Small drinks can now be given, but do not, at this stage, leave water freely available.

KEEP A CHECK ON TEMPERATURE

One of my most valuable pieces of equipment is a clinical thermometer. At the first sign of any trouble, I take the dog's temperature, which, in normal circumstances, should be 101.5 degrees Fahrenheit (38.6°C). I usually smear the end of the thermometer with petroleum jelly and then insert it into the rectum, gently pressing it sideways against the wall of the rectum. If the thermometer is inserted in a straight line, then, more than likely, it will merely be in the middle of a motion not yet excreted, and a correct reading will be almost impossible.

Always be careful to keep hold of the thermometer once inserted into the rectum, as the muscles of the dog's rectum can suck in the thermometer.

I cannot stress too strongly that a rise in temperature above 102.5 degrees Fahrenheit (39.2°C), coupled with any of the above-mentioned symptoms or conditions, is a clear indication that veterinary assistance is needed immediately.

COMMON AILMENTS

Like humans, all dogs are prone to certain ailments, although a fit dog that is fed a well-balanced diet is less likely to be troubled by such complaints. Ideally, your Golden Retriever would only visit the vet once a year for his booster shots. In reality, your dog is more likely to be affected by one of the more common canine ailments, and prompt treatment will ensure a swift recovery.

Anal Glands

If you see your dog dragging his rear end along the floor, or notice a strange smell, his anal glands probably require attention.

These glands are situated at either side of the rectum and, occasionally, they need emptying. The vet will perform this simple operation by squeezing the glands out. Sometimes, they empty themselves when the dog is excited or nervous.

Cystitis

This is caused by inflammation of the bladder. Symptoms include frequent urination, or attempts to do so. If a bitch is affected, there may be evidence of obvious discomfort when she rises from the squatting position.

Cystitis is often the result of an infection, but can be caused by grit, stones, or a growth in the bladder.

Veterinary assistance is a must, and you will need to take a urine sample with you, in a bottle. When the dog or bitch has started to urinate, place a dish under the required spot, and then fill the bottle from the dish. Easy when you know how!

Fortunately, the Golden is a hardy breed, and should suffer few health problems.

False Pregnancy

This condition can occur when a bitch has been in heat, and it will come to light about nine weeks following the heat; the time she would have had her puppies if she had been mated. Symptoms include listlessness, increased thirst and, perhaps, loss of appetite. Milk often appears in the mammary glands and the bitch begins to make her bed for the arrival of the nonexistent puppies. Contact your vet for advice.

Growths

Retrievers, in general, are somewhat prone to growths or tumors. These are more likely to occur in old age, but they can occur in young stock as well. They can range from skin growths to internal tumors, and they can either be benign or malignant. If in doubt, seek veterinary advice immediately.

Kennel Cough

Your dog can be vaccinated (via a nasal spray) against this very

A false pregnancy may occur after a bitch has been in heat.

contagious disease, which can be dangerous in young puppies, or sick or old dogs.

Coughing usually develops five to ten days after contact with an infected animal. A natural breeding ground for this disease is at shows or in boarding kennels, where a number of dogs are gathered together.

Although the dog may appear lively and well, prompt treatment by your vet is essential and, unfortunately, isolation is a necessity.

If you plan to board your dog, he will need to be protected against kennel cough.

BEWARE OF PYOMETRA

This womb infection can be life-threatening. It occurs in unspayed bitches, usually in middle to old age. It often flares up in the period of the estrus cycle known as metestrus, one or two months after the bitch has been in heat. The signs to look for include excessive drinking, increased urination, raised temperature, no appetite, sickness and often the distension of the stomach. Immediate veterinary attention is crucial, and a hysterectomy operation will probably be needed.

HEREDITARY CONDITIONS

The Golden Retriever is a hardy, no-nonsense breed, built on working lines. However, as with most purebred dogs, there are some problems that can arise.

Epilepsy is a condition that needs careful management.

Epilepsy

This is not always an hereditary condition. It is most often seen as a fit or convulsive seizure, which usually occurs when a dog is resting or sleeping.

Symptoms include paddling movements, shaking of the muscles with spasms, and sometimes, involuntary passing of urine. If these symptoms occur, see your vet and give a detailed description of your dog's condition, so that the appropriate treatment can be prescribed.

Eye Conditions

Hereditary cataracts affect some Goldens, but progressive retinal atrophy (PRA) is less common. Your breeder's stock should be free of these conditions; ask to see the eye-testing paperwork to be sure. If you decide to breed, you must get your dog's eyes tested under one of the special programs; ask your vet for details.

Entropion is not as common in Goldens today as it used to be. It occurs when the eyelids turn in, so the eyelashes rub on the cornea, causing the dog great distress. The condition can be recognized from an early age, and surgery is required to correct it.

Heart Conditions

Breeding stock should be screened for Subartic Stenosis (SAS), an hereditary condition that can cause sudden death.

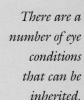

There are a number of eye conditions that can be inherited.

HIP DYSPLASIA (HD)

Most breeds suffer from hip dysplasia to some extent. Even if you bought from a specialized breeder (see Chapter 2), there is no guarantee that your puppy will be free from this condition. HD is an abnormal development of the hip joint. In the United States, Goldens are assessed at 2 years old; they are graded excellent, good, fair, borderline, mildly dysplastic, moderately dysplastic or severely dysplastic. In Canada, Goldens are tested at a minimum of 18 months and receive a pass or fail.

The symptoms of HD appear in a puppy from about 6 months of age. An affected puppy may suffer difficulty or discomfort when getting up from a sitting or lying position; the rear legs may be prone to stiffness or lameness and, when the dog is walking, you may observe a swaying action from side to side of the rear end. The symptoms can most certainly be exacerbated by overexercising and overfeeding.

It is your decision whether or not you have your puppy x-rayed and hip-scored when he is 12 months old. However, if you intend breeding from your dog or bitch, you would be strongly advised to do so.

All breeding stock must be assessed for hip dysplasia

Osteochondrosis

This affects large-sized, fast-growing breeds, including Goldens. It can affect any of the joints, although the elbow joint seems to be most commonly affected in this breed.

Intermittent lameness is first noticed when the puppy is about 4 months of age, and veterinary advice is essential. Surgery can prove successful.

There is some debate as to the cause of this condition; it may be hereditary, but it has also been attributed to excessive supplementation of the diet, overexercise or traumatic episodes.

SUMMARY

It is important for the responsible owner to be aware of the conditions that can affect a dog. But, hopefully, you will have few problems to contend with. As long as your Golden is correctly fed and exercised, and you provide a comprehensive program of preventive health care, he should live a long, happy and healthy life.

With good management, your Golden should live a long and healthy life.